Contents

My name is Megan. These are my friends.

4

My Friends

Paul Humphrey

Photography by Chris Fairclough

W

First published in 2005 by
Franklin Watts
96 Leonard Street
London EC2A 4XD

Franklin Watts Australia
Level 17/207 Kent Street
Sydney NSW 2000

ISBN 0 7496 6172 0 (hbk)
ISBN 0 7496 6184 4 (pbk)

Dewey classification number 302.3'4

A CIP catalogue record for this book is available
from the British Library.

Planning and production by Discovery Books Limited
Editor: Rachel Tisdale
Designer: Ian Winton
Photography: Chris Fairclough
Series advisors: Diana Bentley MA and Dee Reid MA,
Fellows of Oxford Brookes University

The author, packager and publisher would like to thank the following
people for their participation in this book: Mr Skellen and the pupils of
St Peter's Primary School, Harborne; Megan and Mrs Merten-Jones.

Printed in China

5

We sit
together
in school.

We play together
in the playground.

We read books
together.

10

11

We ride our bikes and scooters in the park.

My friend Molly lives next door.

Sometimes I argue with my friends.

Give it back!

After we

argue ...

... we make friends
again.

19

My dog Muffy is a good friend, too.

21

I like all
my friends.

23

Word bank

Look back for these words and pictures.

Argue

Bikes

Books

Dog

Friends

Park

Playground

School

Scooters